CRAZY-O-METER

TEN HAIR-RAISING HAUNTS

by E. C. Andrews

BEARPORT PUBLISHING

Bearport Books, an imprint of Bearport Publishing by FlutterBee

Credits
All images are courtesy of Shutterstock.com, unless otherwise specified. With thanks to Getty Images, Thinkstock Photo, and iStockphoto.

Cover and title page, © eanSablePhotography, Georgios Antonatos, Paul Horia Malaianu; Background pattern throughout, © topform; Recurring, © Kovalov Anatolii; 2–3, © Dan Bridge; 4–5, © FOTOKITA, Sven Hansche; 6–7, © BRO.vector, Kent Weakley, Nagel Photography; 8–9, © notkoo, Daniel Marian, klyaksun; 10–11, © MaryValery, JeanSablePhotography, Zeynep Demir Aslim, StockSmartStart, Kobee, Iryna Palmina; 12–13, © Taber Photographic Co. (I.W. Taber), Public domain, via Wikimedia Commons, Agor2012, DreamArt123, JosepPerianes; 14–15, © Prasit Rithtem, Yulia M, Howard Pyle, Public domain, via Wikimedia Commons, Sarah Jennie; 16–17, © FRIEVA, CassielMx, doleesi; 18–19, © Violet Sun, Wirestock Creators, Pandora Pictures, Yaran; 20–21, © Hennadii H, ahkhamr, Victoria Nevzorova, lemono, Zbigniew Guzowski, Sergii Figurnyi; 22–23, © Anatolir, Vitezslav Halamka, Gandolfo Cannatella, Public domain, via Wikimedia Commons, NishanDesigns.

Bearport Publishing Company Product Development Team
Kayla Eggert, Theresa Emminizer, Kim Jones, Allison Juda, Cole Nelson, Naomi Reich, Steve Scheluchin, Tiana Tran

Library of Congress Cataloging-in-Publication Data is available at www.loc.gov or upon request from the publisher.

ISBN: 979-8-89577-607-0 (hardcover)
ISBN: 979-8-89577-695-7 (ebook)

For more information, write to Bearport Publishing, 3500 American Blvd W, Suite 150, Bloomington, MN 55431.
Printed in the United States of America.

CONTENTS

HORRIBLE HAIR-RAISERS

History is full of scary and spooky stories. Let's take a look back at some truly haunting events. How ghostly do they get?

THE GREENWICH FOOT TUNNEL

WHEN: **1902** WHERE: **London, England**

People wishing to cross under the River Thames can do so using the Greenwich Foot Tunnel . . . if they dare. Numerous reports say that a ghostly Victorian couple can sometimes be seen walking through the tunnel arm in arm before disappearing into thin air.

Other chilling tunnel experiences include hearing voices and feeling sudden drops in **temperature**.

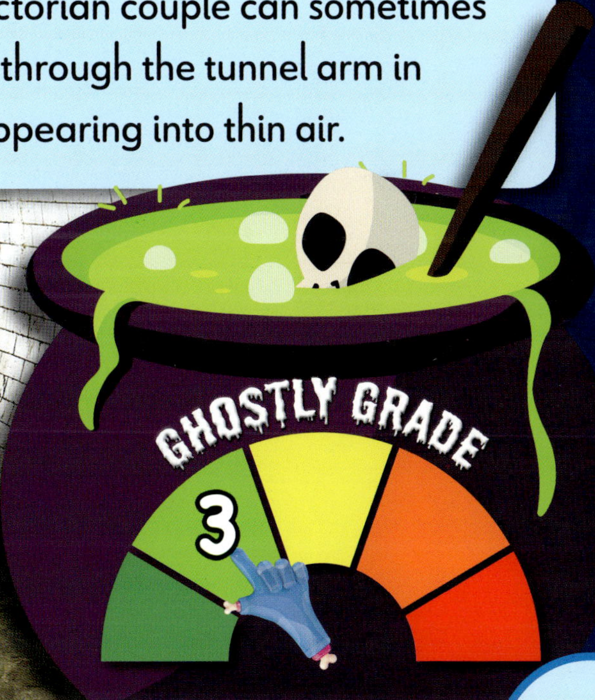

ST. AUGUSTINE LIGHTHOUSE

WHEN: **1850s** WHERE: **St. Augustine, Florida**

Being up in a lighthouse all night can get lonely. But what if you had some company? The St. Augustine Lighthouse is thought to be haunted by several spirits.

At the lighthouse, some people have heard doors opening and closing by themselves.

One spirit is said to be a lighthouse keeper who died following a nasty fall. Some say he continues to watch over the tower to this day. Other reports mention three ghostly girls giggling in the night.

HOIA BACIU FOREST

WHEN: **1400s** WHERE: **Transylvania, Romania**

The Hoia Baciu forest is an eerie place. It is said to be named after a shepherd. He mysteriously disappeared, along with all 200 of his sheep, after entering the forest.

Could it be aliens? Some reports mention UFO sightings in the forest.

Locals also tell a story about a little girl who disappeared into the forest—only to return five years later. She still wore the same clothes! Even stranger, the girl didn't know how much time had passed.

HIGHGATE CEMETERY

WHEN: **1839** WHERE: **London, England**

About 170,000 people are buried in Highgate Cemetery, which makes it the perfect hotspot for ghostly encounters. Some haunting stories include tales of a creepy devil and a floating nun.

The spookiest **legend** tells of the Highgate Vampire. People have reported seeing a tall figure with red eyes gliding over the graves. He is said to leave dead animals in his wake.

When the vampire is near, some report feeling cold and having their clocks stop working.

THE WINCHESTER HOUSE

WHEN: **1884** WHERE: **San Jose, California**

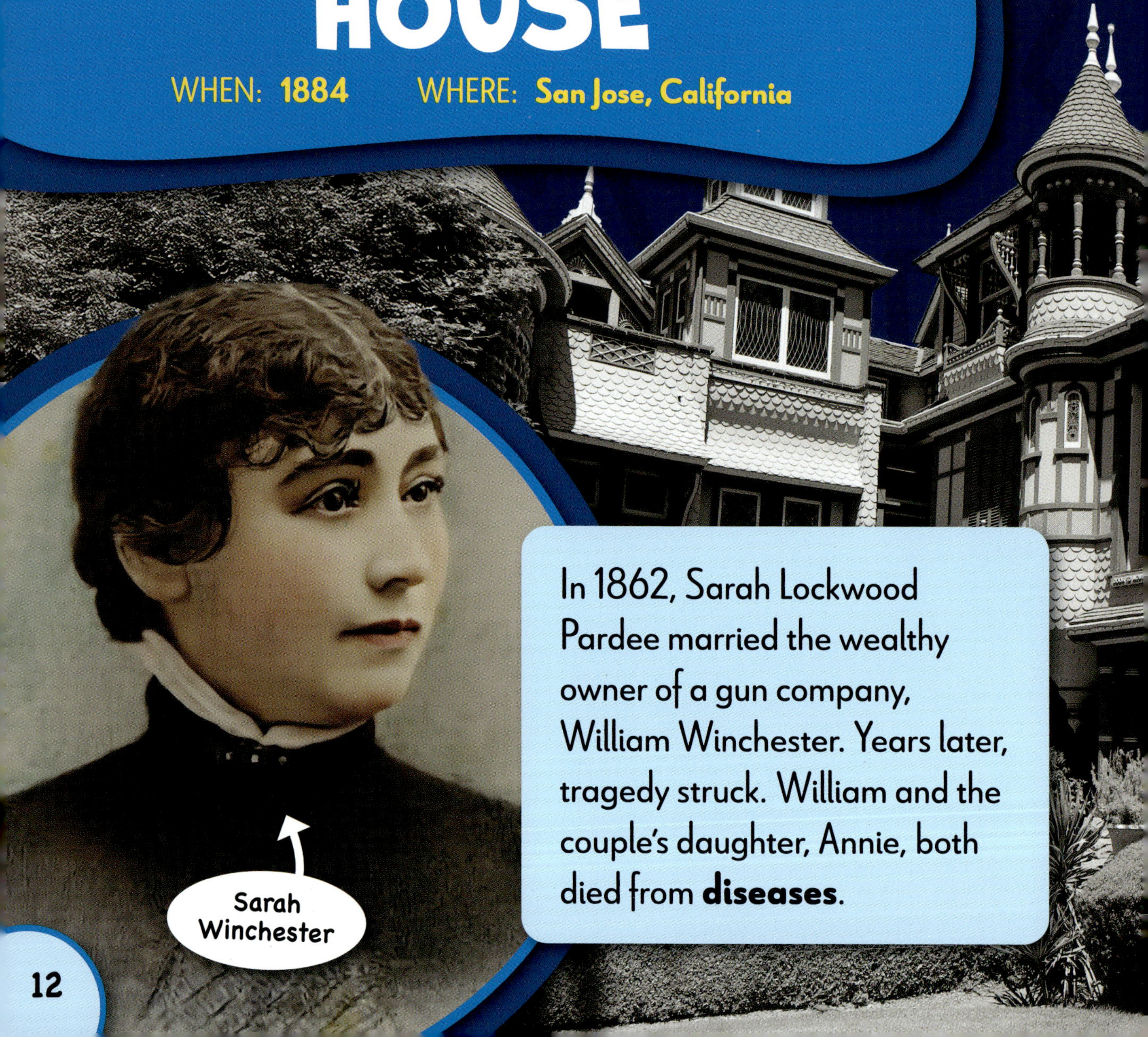

In 1862, Sarah Lockwood Pardee married the wealthy owner of a gun company, William Winchester. Years later, tragedy struck. William and the couple's daughter, Annie, both died from **diseases**.

From that moment on, Sarah believed she was being haunted by the angry spirits of those killed by guns from William's company. To stay safe, she built new rooms in her house for 38 years! Sarah thought the hammering sounds would scare the ghosts away.

Sarah also built odd doors that led to walls and stairways into ceilings.

THE TOWN OF SALEM

WHEN: **1690s** WHERE: **Salem, Massachusetts**

Many people dress up as witches for Halloween. However, if someone said you were a witch in the 17th century, you were in big trouble!

In the small town of Salem, three girls **accused** a local woman of witchcraft. Soon after, more were accused. About 200 were called witches, and 19 of them were hanged.

ISLA DE LAS MUÑECAS

WHEN: **1950s** WHERE: **Xochimilco, Mexico**

One horrific day, the caretaker of Isla de las Muñecas found the dead body of a little girl and her doll floating in the water. To comfort her angry spirit, he hung the doll in a tree.

In Spanish, *Isla de las Muñecas* means Island of the Dolls.

The man continued collecting dolls and hanging them up all over the island until the day he was found dead in the exact place where the girl drowned. Some people say they now hear the dolls whispering to one another.

POVEGLIA ISLAND

WHEN: **1300s** WHERE: **Venice, Italy**

Poveglia Island is known as the Island of Ghosts. It was first used as a graveyard for people who died of the **plague**. But that all changed during the 20th century.

The island is now **abandoned**. However, some say they can still hear the hospital bell ringing . . .

In 1922, the island became a hospital where a doctor performed horrible human experiments. Because of its spine-chilling history, many people believe the island is filled with unhappy spirits.

Inside Poveglia's hospital

KING TUTANKHAMUN'S CURSE

WHEN: **1922** **WHERE:** **Luxor, Egypt**

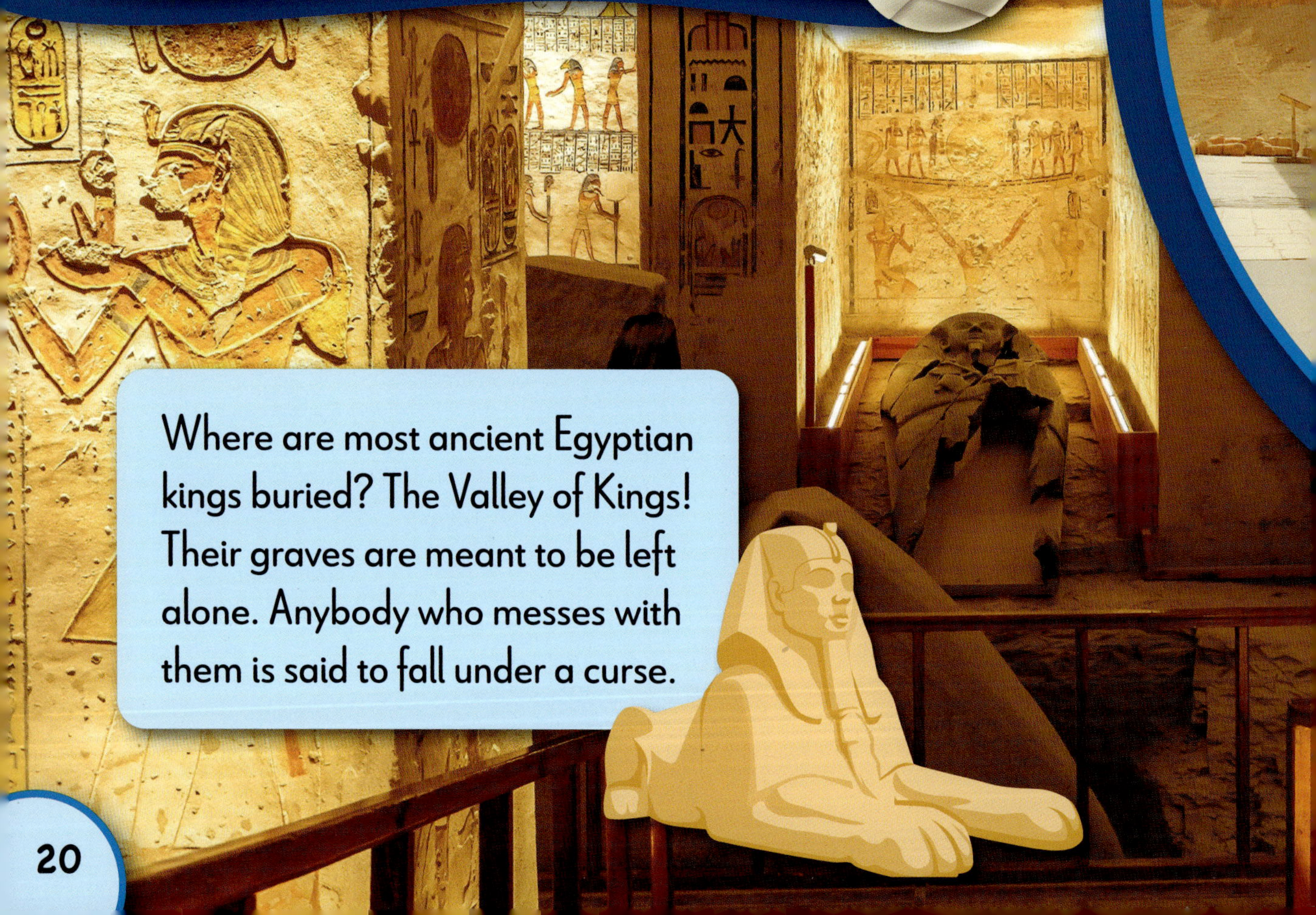

Where are most ancient Egyptian kings buried? The Valley of Kings! Their graves are meant to be left alone. Anybody who messes with them is said to fall under a curse.

The **archaeologists** who disturbed the grave of King Tutankhamun mysteriously died soon afterward. Some people thought this was a punishment from the angry king. It has become known as Tutankhamun's curse.

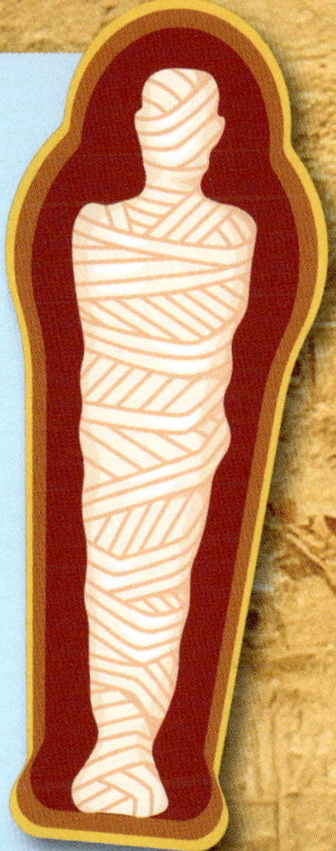

Some people say they have seen the ghost of an Egyptian king riding through the Valley of the Kings in a **chariot**.

THE CAPUCHIN CATACOMBS

WHEN: **1599** WHERE: **Sicily, Italy**

The Capuchin Catacombs of Palermo are underground tunnels that contain **mummified** remains. There were nearly 8,000 corpses placed there. Among them is a girl named Rosalia Lombardo.

Rosalia died in 1920. She was mummified so perfectly that she looks like she's sleeping. Some people said they have seen Rosalia blink!

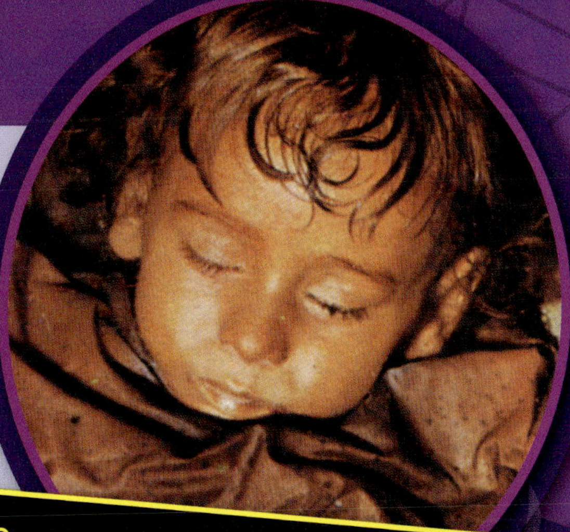

People call Rosalia the blinking mummy, the sleeping angel, or the sleeping beauty of Palermo.

GLOSSARY

abandoned empty or no longer used

accused blamed for doing something wrong

archaeologists people who dig up objects and the remains of people who lived in the past

chariot a two-wheeled cart pulled by horses

diseases illnesses

legend a story from the past that is often not entirely true

mummified prepared so a body lasts a long time

plague a deadly illness that spreads very quickly

temperature how hot or cold something is

INDEX